Author biography

Amaresh Nath (Co-founder and COO): He is a Ph.D. scholar at TISS, Mumbai, and also the Head of Research and Designs at Aatma Prakash Mental Health Foundation. He has been in the field of psychology for the past 14 years and a mental health practitioner for the past 7+ years, during which he has conducted over 300 workshops, and taken above 7500 counselling sessions. He also has been a faculty member at TISS, Guwahati, and Pune Institute of Business Management, Pune. He specializes in positive solutions to problems and a gestalt school of thought.

Harish Bhuvan (Co-founder and CEO): He is the Founder of Compassionate Clowns - A Non-profit dedicated to the wellbeing of distressed human beings in the hospital. He is a two times TEDx speaker and Guinness World Record Holder. His approach to therapeutic clowning has touched thousands of volunteers and patients alike. By profession, he is a psychologist and taken above 15000 counselling sessions during the 8 years of his experience.

CONTENTS

Experiential Exercises and Activities for Group and Individual Work

Blending Psychology and Fun

Amaresh Nath and Harish Bhuvan

ISBN 978-93-5458-462-6
© Amaresh Nath and Harish Bhuvan 2021
Published in India 2021 by Pencil

A brand of
One Point Six Technologies Pvt. Ltd.
123, Building J2, Shram Seva Premises,
Wadala Truck Terminal, Wadala (E)
Mumbai 400037, Maharashtra, INDIA
E connect@thepencilapp.com
W www.thepencilapp.com

DISCLAIMER: *The opinions expressed in this book are those of the authors and do not purport to reflect the views of the Publisher.*

About the Organization

A dream that one can fulfil on their own, is a plan, one for which one needs the help of many, is a revolution, but a dream that is shared with the whole world, for it requires the help of the whole population to fulfilled, is a revolution! And we at Whaterr Solutions dream of a revolution in the field of mental health!

Founded on 14/09/2020, by Mr. Harish Bhuvan and Dr. Amaresh Nath, Whaterr Solutions is a one-stop destination for both mental health professionals and the general public alike, to cater to their various mental health needs.

We are on a mission to destigmatize mental health and make mental health care a part of every individual's daily routine. We provide our services in four different ways:

- We offer specific specialized counselling services by well-qualified experts

- Tailor-made Diploma courses in Psychology

- Workshops, seminars, and webinars on mental health and wellness

- We support that with a daily series of free online activities which are open for the public to attend on Mental health and Wellness

With innovation at our core, we strive to make mental health accessible and understandable for all and one of our USPs is to add an element of variance in all that we do; whether it is our approach of providing psychotherapy or any other unique activities.

About the Book

More often than not we perform everyday activities without realizing that they have a therapeutic effect. This book is a collection of activities that are either original creations of the authors or original reinterpretations of popular games and activities. Some activities are designed purely for group work, some are purely designed for individual work, some can be used for both individual and group work, and some can be used as techniques of self-help. The effectiveness of each activity has been verified by the authors over their careers.

This book is an attempt to blend psychology with an element of fun to promote sound mental health. The exercises and activities in the book are intended to provide an experience of self-discovery and insight generation.

Who is it meant for?

This book is primarily meant for mental health professionals who do individual and group therapy, and/or trainers who provide soft skills training. This book can however be also used as a self-help book for anyone interested in their own mental wellbeing.

What the book is not?

This book is not meant to be a replacement for conventional therapy. And if used as a self-help book, it is not meant to be a replacement for a counselling session.

Topics covered

The exercises presented through this book revolve around topics of communication, anger management, relationship management, problem-solving, self-esteem, goal setting, team building, self-control, empathy, interpersonal issues, subliminal perception, resilience building, addiction, self-development, resource management, moving on, time management, among others.

How to use the book?

Each activity presented in the book has the following common sections:

Introduction:A brief about what the activity is about.

Most suitable context: Settings where the activity can bring forth optimum results.

Materials:A list of items that are required to conduct the activity.

Preparation: Certain preparatory steps before conducting the activity.

Instructions: Instructions to be delivered to the participants.

Debrief: Understanding the experience of the participants and clarifying to them why the activity was conducted. It is to be noted here that the "debrief" section is a guideline and the facilitator doesn't have to stick to every word.

Abbreviations used in the book

O:The exercise is meant to be used for a one-on-one (individual/couple) therapeutic setting

G:The exercise is meant to be used in a group setting (workshop, group therapy, and/or family therapy)

O&G/G&O: The exercise can be used in both individual and group settings

SH: The exercise can be used for self-help purposes

Blow the Candle (G&O)

Introduction

This is an activity that can be used in various contexts; ideally in a group setting, but can be used for individual sessions as well. It is a powerful tool for generating insight among the participants. It is however to be kept in mind that if someone has breathing problems, it is better for them not to participate in this activity as it involves a restriction of one's breathing.

Most suitable contexts

Workshops on communication, relationship management, anger management, and/or problem-solving.

Materials

- Candles (1 per person)

- Lighter/Matches

- Scarves (2 per person)

Preparation

Make the participants stand in a manner that each participant has a candle in front of them.

Instructions

- Light the candle in front of you and take two steps backward.

- Fold one scarf into a rectangle the size of your face and use the other scarf to tie it over your entire face.

- Turn around where you are standing three times.

- With your hands at your back, try to blow out the candle in front of you.

- Now rearrange your scarves so that you can see and try to blow out your candle.

- Now remove the folded scarf and put on the single scarf over your nose and mouth.

- Once again try to blow out the candle in front of you.

- Remove your scarf and blow out the candle.

Debrief

- ***Communication:*** The candle is something we want to address and the scarves are the various obstacles in the process of communication. In the first scenario, we are clueless about our actions; we plan a conversation in our heads but don't speak out due to various fears; here it is important to emphasize the fact nobody can read minds and if we want to express something, we need to say it out, whether through words, actions, or both. In the second and third scenarios, we tried expressing but were not clear in our attempt. Then finally we removed all our resistances and expressed what we want, thus the candle was blown out and the task was completed. (In case somebody manages to blow the candle before the fourth scenario: sometimes we do manage to express despite the obstacles but without the obstacles, the process is much simpler, however that doesn't mean that we stop trying).

- ***Intimacy:*** Fear, jealousy, doubt, pride, etc. are various barriers that prevent us from getting close with someone, and the more resistances we drop, the closer we get to others. Here candle represents the other person and the scarves, the various resistances that we have and in the first scenario, the resistances were too high and it was impossible to connect with the other person, then in the second and third scenario we dropped some of our resistances, but we were not able to connect that deeply, then finally in the fourth scenario, we dropped all our resistances and connected with the other person on an intimate level.

- ***Task completion:*** The three biggest barriers in the path of completing a task are not knowing what the task is, procrastination, and improper planning; the biggest threat is not knowing about the task, which leaves us clueless in the dark. Next is procrastination; when one procrastinates, the task is completely left untouched, thus in the second scenario, the candle which signified the task, was left untouched. A lesser threat, but a significant obstacle nevertheless is improper planning, where one does attempt to perform the task but is not able to perform at their optimum, thus the candle fluttered, but was not blown out. Finally, when we removed all the barriers and performed the task on time in a planned manner, the candle was blown out and the task was completed.

- ***Anger:*** Anger, if not managed or channeled in a healthy manner, prevents us from doing anything. In the first scenario, the level of anger was too high and we were blinded by it; losing sight of what is actually happening. In the second scenario, we are still experiencing raw emotions, due to which we were unable to perform our task. In the third scenario, we began to keep our anger in control, so we managed to perform our task, but our emotions were still preventing us from performing in an optimum level. Finally, we had gained full control of our anger and managed to perform the task with ease.

Poison and Elixer (O&G)

Introduction

Based on the technique of visualization, this activity is ideally most effective for individual sessions, but can also be used for group sessions, and as a self-help technique. Even though it is most effective when used with props, but in cases of unavailability of props (especially when being used as a self-help technique), this activity can be done purely through visualization. This exercise has two variants; one suitable for a formal setting, and the other for a more informal/more accommodating setting.

Most suitable contexts

Workshops/individual sessions for emotion management and self-esteem.

Materials

Empty plastic bottles (two per person)

Preparation

Hand two empty bottles to each participant.

Instructions

1. (In case of unavailability of bottles) Imagine there are two empty plastic bottles in front of you.

2. Pick up one of the bottles with both your hands and close your eyes.

3. Recollect all the times when you have been angry, upset, scared, or experienced any other negative emotions.

4. Feel all the experiences these emotions induce; do not try to resist.

5. Now imagine all your emotions and experiences turning into a liquid.

6. Let this liquid slowly fill up the bottle in your hand; it is okay if it overflows.

7. Once your feel that the bottle is full and you don't have any more liquid to put into it, crush it with all the might you can muster.

8. Keep crushing the bottle till it can't be crushed anymore.

9. Drop the bottle, take a deep breath, and open your eyes.

10. Pick up the other bottle and close your eyes.

11. Recollect all the times when you were happy, felt successful, hopeful, or experienced any other positive emotions.

12. Feel all the experiences these emotions induce; do not try to resist.

13. Now imagine all your emotions and experiences turning into a liquid.

14. Let this liquid slowly fill up the bottle in your hand; it is okay if it overflows, in fact, let it overflow if it does.

15. Once your feel that the bottle is full and you don't have any more liquid to put into it, drink the liquid slowly till you empty the bottle.

16. Experience the warmth as the liquid flows within you.

17. Once you feel ready, open your eyes.

Debrief

- Emotions are but a form of energy that is stored within us if not released. Through our positive and negative experiences, we experience positive and negative emotions, which in turn generate positive and negative energies respectively within us. We release our energy when we talk or perform any action. But we release positive energy more easily than negative energy, which can be due to various social influences, and as a result, negative energies are stored within us. If the negativity within us exceeds the positivity, various problems begin to arise.

- This activity can be practiced anytime, anywhere to maintain a balance of positive and negative energies within us. Remember, no matter how much we look for it around us, all the positivity that we need is within us; we just need to remind ourselves from time to time of the same.

Variant (for informal/more accommodating settings)
Materials

- A small bottle of orange juice (1 per participant)

- A small, plastic bottle of green colored water (1 per participant)

- Balloons (1 per participant)

- Funnels (1 per participant)

Preparation (phase 1)

Hand each of the participants one balloon, a funnel, and a bottle of green water.

Instructions

1. Take the bottle with both your hands and close your eyes.

2. Recollect all the times when you have been angry, upset, scared, or experienced any other negative emotions.

3. Feel all the experiences these emotions induce; do not try to resist.

4. Now imagine all your emotions and experiences turning into a liquid.

5. Let this liquid slowly fill up the bottle in your hand; it is okay if it overflows.

6. Once you are satisfied filling the bottle, open your eyes.

7. Take the funnel and transfer the contents of the bottle into the balloon.

8. Once the bottle is empty, crush the bottle with all your might and throw the crushed bottle away with all the might you can muster.

9. Take the filled-up balloon between your hands and burst it.

Preparation (phase 2)

Hand each of the participants a bottle of orange juice.

Instructions

1. Take the bottle with both your hands and close your eyes.

2. Recollect all the times when you were happy, felt successful, hopeful, or experienced any other positive emotions.

3. Feel all the experiences these emotions induce; do not try to resist.

4. Now imagine all your emotions and experiences turning into a liquid.

5. Let this liquid slowly fill up the bottle in your hand; it is okay if it overflows, in fact, let it overflow if it does.

6. Once your feel that the bottle is full and you don't have any more liquid to put into it, drink the liquid slowly till you empty the bottle.

7. Experience the sweetness of the liquid as it flows within you.

8. Once you feel ready, open your eyes.

Debrief

Emotions are but a form of energy that is stored within us if not released. Through our positive and negative experiences, we experience positive and negative emotions, which in turn generate positive and negative energies respectively within us. We release our energy when we talk or perform any action. But we release positive energy more easily than negative energy, which can be due to various social influences, and as a result, negative energies are stored within us. If the negativity within us exceeds the positivity, various problems begin to arise. It is important to address the source of the negative emotions (the first bottle, in this case), and once the source is taken care of, the remnants (the balloon, in this case) is easy to be removed from our lives. Unlike the negative energies, which need to be expelled from the system, positive energies within us need to be occasionally kept replenished by reminding ourselves of the same (the way you drank the orange juice).

Fly High (O&G, SH)

Introduction

At different points of our lives, most of us have flown paper planes; sometimes for casual pleasure and sometimes with a competitive spirit. This activity reverse-engineers the process of flying a paper plane from a philosophical perspective to generate insights. Even though ideal for group settings, it can also be used in individual sessions and as a self-help technique.

Most suitable context

Workshops/individual sessions on planning and goal setting.

Materials

- Sheets of paper (1 per person)

- Pens (1 per person)

Preparation

Hand a sheet of paper and a pen to each participant.

Instructions

1. On your sheet of paper, put down the dreams and aspirations that you wish to fulfil in the future.

2. You can write down in points, or in paragraphs, or if you feel like, you can also draw your dream on the sheet of paper.

3. Once you are done, fold your paper into an aeroplane, and write your name on the plane; if you want, you can also decorate the plane.

4. Now make it fly and see how far it goes.

Debrief

Just as we had to launch the paper plane to make it fly, for our ambitions to fulfil, we need to take certain steps. You might have noticed that the planes that did not receive sufficient elevation and/or thrust during taking off, fell down fast; this can be drawn similarity to when we are not motivated enough to reach our dreams or when we do not dream big enough. In this case, the plane did not have enough fuel to go the distance. Similarly, you might have also noticed that the planes that had too high an elevation and/or too much thrust, did not travel too far either. This can be drawn similarity to situations where we either dream beyond our capacities or get to excited and undertake rash decisions; we might reach great heights, but we don't go the distance and fall really hard. On the other hand, the planes that went the maximum distance, had the right amount of elevation and thrust; thus, it is important to have dreams that are big but not too big for our capacities and undertake suitable and wise steps to ensure that our dreams are converted into reality.

The Missing Jigsaw (G)

Introduction
As children and even as adults we have played with jigsaw puzzles. Even though a fun game, this puzzle can be a source of wisdom regarding interpersonal relationships and teamwork. This activity highlights how the process of solving a jigsaw puzzle can be a learning experience.

Most suitable context
Workshops on team building and teamwork.

Materials
A jigsaw puzzle set

Preparation
From the set, give four participants a piece each and tell them not to tell the others that they have pieces of the puzzle.

Instructions

1. Try to complete the picture of the jigsaw puzzle in front of you, you have 10 minutes to complete the task.

2. (Once the task is complete) Use the missing pieces to fill the gaps.

Debrief

A team is as strong as the members and when even a single participant decides not to participate, or goes missing, the dynamics of the entire team is impacted. Another beauty of a team is that it gives space for every member to pool in their strengths and cover up the weaknesses of a single member with the strengths of the others. The four missing pieces are just like members of a team; they are all unique and help to complete the picture.

London Statue (G)

Introduction

A popular game among young children and a party activity among young adults (among whom it is popularly known as the mannequin challenge), this activity highlights the importance of working together, thinking outside the box, and remaining calm in the face of adversity.

Most suitable context

Workshops on teamwork, creative problem solving, and self-control.

Materials

Chits containing "actors" and "reactors"

Preparation

Make the participants pick a chit each.

Instructions

1. On your chits, you will see that it is written either "actor" or "reactor".

2. The actors come together on one side and reactors come together on the other side.

3. The actors shall close their eyes and say "L.O.N.D.O.N, London statue!"

4. While the actors have their eyes closed, the reactors can do anything, but once they say "statue", you all have to freeze on your spot.

5. While the reactors are frozen, the actors, your task is to make them move; you can make them laugh, irritate them, scare them, etc.

6. But remember that the actors need to make the reactors react without touching them in any way.

7. While the actors try to make you react, the reactors have to hold their positions and try not to react.

8. The only form of reaction that can be excused is the blinking of the eyes.

Debrief

- Reactors, how did you feel when you were trying not to react?

- And actors, how did you feel when the reactors were not reacting? Did you have an urge to physically touch the reactors?

- Sometimes we do not get what we want or things do not go the way we had planned, and it is times like that when we need to ensure that we remain calm and do not give in to our impulses.

- Sometimes it also happens that we are in certain social situations where it is better to either not respond or try to avoid it; the situation can be either positive (for example friends call us a party but we have an exam coming), or negative (for example somebody insults us).

- It is important that we assess the situation, evaluate options, and act accordingly instead of reacting impulsively.

Doctor-Doctor, Please Help Us! (G)

Introduction

Based on a popular childhood game, also known as "human knot", this activity pushes participants to situations where they have to work together and think out of the box. It brings forth both a competitive spirit and team spirit as well among the participants.

Most suitable context

Workshops on team building and creative problem-solving.

Materials

Chits (1 per participant)

Preparation

- On one of the chits, write "doctor", "assistant" on two others, and "patient" on the rest.

- Make the participants pick up a chit each.

Instructions

1. The "doctor" and "assistant" please stand aside and close your eyes.

2. The rest of you please form a circle by holding each other's hands.

3. Now, without breaking the circle, tangle yourselves up; you can go below the hands, go above them, etc. as long as you don't break the circle.

4. Once you are done entangling yourself, call out "doctor, doctor, come and please help us!"

5. Now the doctor and assistant open your eyes and try to untangle the group and restore them to the original circle.

6. Remember that while you are untangling them, you can try anything but cannot make them leave each other's hands.

Debrief

- What do you think was the purpose of this activity?

- While the patients coordinated among themselves to create the most complicated tangled up formation, the doctor and the assistants tried to solve the puzzle and untangle you all.

- This is how teamwork works; we all put in our resources (our time, energy, skills, or any other resources) to make sure that the team succeeds.

- We might be very capable individuals, but no matter how capable we are, there are times when we need the help of others, and there is no shame in seeking the help of other whenever the need arises.

- It is also important to keep things simple as possible as if things become complicated, it becomes difficult to untangle; thus, it is important to practice the virtues of trust and honesty to ensure that things remain simple.

Water Filter (O&G)

Introduction

This is an activity that is equally effective in both individual and group settings and is a simple yet powerful means of generating insights. Since the activity involves water, it is advisable that the participants are intimated in prior of the possibilities of getting wet.

Most suitable context

Workshops/individual sessions on problem-solving

Materials

- Scarves/handkerchief (1 per person)

- A glass of water (1 per person)

Preparation

Hand each participant a scarf and a glass of water each.

Instructions

1. Take the scarf and tie it over your lips in a manner that it is tight enough to be stretched but lose enough that you can move your lips; do not fold it and let the excess hang down.

2. Try drinking from the glass of water; don't take small sips but drink like you normally would.

3. Now remove the scarf and put it over the mouth of the glass.

4. Once again try drinking the water.

Debrief

- Did you notice any difference in the two scenarios?

- Unlike the first scenario where quite some water was spilt, it was almost like normally drinking water in the second scenario.

- Why do you think this happened?

- In the first scenario, the problem wasn't directly addressed, and hence a lot of resources got wasted.

- But in the second scenario, since the problem was addressed at the root, there was less or no wastage of resources.

- Which scenario is more resembling of your approach toward problem solving?

- Hence it is always advisable, when it comes to problem solving, to take a direct approach and address the problem itself rather than simply taking protective measures.

Do Not Touch Your Knot (G&O)

Introduction

In this world of cutthroat competition, there is a general tendency to ignore what people around us are going on, and with the fear of our weaknesses being exploited, we often keep our problems to ourselves. This activity can be done in two variants; one for a group setting, and another for individual sessions. It is however to be kept in mind that if someone has breathing problems, it is better for them not to participate in this activity as it involves a restriction of one's
breathing.

Most suitable context

As part of group settings, this exercise is effective for workshops on community and team building, empathy, and communication. If used in an individual setting, it is ideal to be used mid-session, when a client begins to show resistance, to help them understand the need to open up and address their issues.

Materials

Scarves (3 per participant)

Pre-preparation

Bring the participants out of the room/space and hand

them each three scarves.

Instructions

1. Roughly fold one scarf to the size of your face.

2. Place it on the other scarf and tie it over your face like a mask covering your entire face reaching across the top of your head above and neck below.

3. Make sure that the knot is tight and secure it with a second knot.

4. Use the third scarf as a frame for your mask; covering everything except the face portion and tie two knots below the chin.

Preparation

Holding their hands, one by one bring all the participants back into the room and make them stand at random places

Instructions

1. You can now remove your masks but remember two things; you cannot touch your own knot, and you cannot say a single word.

2. If at any point in time you feel it is getting too hard to manage with the mask, just raise your hand and I shall come to help you out.

3. However, try to continue with the activity till I say stop.

4. (After 5 minutes) You may now untie your own knots.

Debrief

- How did you all feel during the activity?

- Just as it got more and more uncomfortable with passing time, problems also continue to get worse if not addressed on time.

- There are times when we alone cannot handle our problems, and during times like that it is perfectly alright to seek the help of others; if we stay silent nobody will know the pain, we are going through.

- Most often there are people around us who are suffering just like, but neither of us realizes that because they are silent about their problems and we blind to theirs, and vice-versa. Thus, we continue to suffer alone when we can all work together to lift each up and rise together.

- Any problem, unless addressed at the roots (the knots in this case), cannot be solved.

<u>Variant (for an individual session)</u>

Materials

2 scarves

Instructions

1. Roughly fold one scarf to the size of your face

2. Place it on the other scarf and tie it over your face like a mask covering your entire face reaching across the top of your head above and neck below.

3. Make sure that the knot is tight and secure it with a second knot (if there is enough scarf, tie the second knot below your chin).

4. Try to keep this mask on for as long as you can or until I tell you to.

5. If you want, you can lower the mask for short breathers, but do not touch the knots.

Procedure

-   Once the client is done tying the scarf, resume the counselling process.

-   If the client expresses suffocation, ask them if they can continue for a while longer; if they can't, allow them to remove it.

-   Engage them in the counselling process in a manner that they are distracted from the fact that their face is covered.

-   Considering that they haven't removed the scarves, allow them to remove them after ten minutes.

Debrief

- How did you feel while you had your face covered?

- What were the various emotions you experienced?

- How many times did you find yourself trying to lower the mask?

- How did it make you feel when you couldn't lower it?

- Just as it got more and more uncomfortable with passing time, problems also continue to get worse if not addressed on time.

- Any problem, unless addressed at the roots (the knots in this case), cannot be solved; the wrong approach often leads to failure, which in turn leads to frustration.

Video Call (O)

Introduction

Mirrors are a piece of powerful equipment when it comes to therapy; it has been used in various settings to address varied issues. This activity is a variant of the popular "Empty Chair" technique that is commonly used by therapists who practice gestalt therapy; the client shall have to imagine conversing with the "concerned other" just like in the classic version of the technique, but in this variant, instead of visualizing with their eyes closed, they shall have access to both visual and auditory stimuli.

Most suitable context

Individual counselling sessions involving addressing interpersonal issues.

Prerequisite

- A conventional counselling setting where there is a desk in front of the client's seat. If the setting is unconventional, make the client sit in front of a table.

- This technique is to be used once the "concerned other(s)" with whom communication needs to take place, are identified over the counselling session(s).

Materials

- A mirror

- A long scarf/dupatta

- A pair of radio walkie-talkies (or a pair of cellphones if walkie-talkies are unavailable).

Preparation

- Ask the client to close their eyes.

- Hand them the scarf and ask them to cover their face in a manner only their eyes are exposed.

- While they put on the scarf arrange the mirror on the desk/table in a manner that the maximum view on the mirror is up to their shoulders.

- Hand them one walkie-talkie and place the other behind the mirror (in case of using cellphones, ask them to take out their cell phone and keep your cell phone behind the mirror, but keep the one behind the mirror on complete silent mode).

- In case of cellphones: With their permission, use their phone to dial your number, and once it rings, answer it, put it on speakerphone and hand them back their phone (to ensure optimum efficiency, ask them to keep their phone unlocked before starting the entire procedure).

- Ask them to open their eyes.

Instructions (before asking them to open their eyes)

1. When you open your eyes, imagine that you are on a video call with X (name of the concerned other).

2. Tell him/her all that you have been wanting to say for all this while; let out all your thoughts and emotions.

3. Also, try putting yourself in their shoes and respond to yourself the way they might if you had actually said to them in real life.

4. Try continuing with the conversation between the both of you as long as you can.

5. Once you are done with the conversation, end it like you would end it in real, put the screen down, and remove your scarf.

Note

Encourage the client and prompt whenever required to ensure they have a full-fledged conversation.

Debrief

Ask them how they feel after the experience and pick up the rest of the session from what they share and your observations during the exercise.

Chaos (G)

Introduction

When working in a team, one comes across various barriers that hinder the performance of the entire group, and it is important to identify and address these issues for the team to operate optimally. This is a group activity suited ideally for a corporate/organizational setup and is a powerful tool to generate insight regarding interpersonal dynamics.

Most suitable context

Workshops on team building and communication

Materials

- Sheets of paper (1 per participant)

- Pens (1 per participant)

- Pairs of scissors (1 per participant)

- Glasses of water (1 per participant)

- Plastic bags (2 per participant)

- Chits (1 per participant)

Preparation

- Divide the participants into pairs.

- Ask them to chose either role A or role B within the pairs.

- On the chits, write simple tasks like "write your name", "cut a circle", "draw a flower", etc.; it is ok if certain tasks are repeated.

- Call the participants playing role B aside, ask them to pick a chit, and hand them a glass of water.

- Put a plastic bag over the fists of each of the participants playing role A, and hand them a sheet of paper, a pen, and a pair of scissors.

Instructions

1. All the B's have received a chit containing a particular task; you have to instruct your partner to perform that task.

2. But before giving the instructions, take a big sip of water and give the instructions with your mouth full.

3. Remember, you can only orally give the instructions; no gestures are permitted.

4. All the A's likewise shall have to comprehend what their partner is saying and perform that task using the tools given to you.

Debrief

- All those giving instructions, how was your experience?

- All those following instructions, how was your experience?

- Whenever we work in a team, we usually experience two major hurdles; improper delivery of instructions and/or implementation of instructions by unskilled hands.

- Here the water in your mouth is an analogy of all the various barriers one faces while delivering instructions; whether it is difficulty in articulation, poor grasp of the matter to be delivered, or any other such difficulties.

- While the bagged hands are an analogy for the inability to perform the task, which might be due to various reasons like physical limitations, lack of skills regarding the particular task, or any other such difficulties.

- For a group to perform optimally, it is essential that all the members are well equipped to ensure that the group operates smoothly.

Daily Fortune (SH)

Introduction

This activity is about the psychological concepts of self-fulfilling prophecy, wherein an individual acts in a particular manner so as to prove a certain statement(s) to be true (but more often than not, this is done unconsciously), and subliminal perception, wherein an individual receives certain information from the environment and begins to process it in a way that it begins to impact their conscious thoughts and actions without them realizing about the piece of information that they had picked up. Try this little experiment and see if it makes your day a little better.

Procedure

Almost all of us keep daily newspapers, and in the newspaper, there is a daily section for the day's horoscope. After waking up in the morning, as soon as possible (before you might get any other information), ask someone to read your horoscope (but not aloud), and then ask that person if the reading is positive or negative. If the reading is positive, ask the person to read it aloud for you, and if it is a negative reading, let it be, do not listen to it. If you were told that the reading is negative, go through the reading at the end of the day to see if your day really was as negative as it was written there.

Debrief

- The reason I am saying to attend to the horoscope in the morning is that, during that time, our mind is fresh and more receptive to information. And since our horoscope is a personal message, it is very likely to play at the back of our mind throughout the day, thus, making very subtle influences on our thoughts and actions; in other words, we unconsciously make attempts to make what we read in the horoscope to come true in some form or another. So, after hearing a positive horoscope reading, we are more likely to work towards making a good day. Yes, it is possible that our horoscope had predicted an extremely awesome day for us, and we might not have had that awesome a day, but if we retrospect and reflect upon that particular day, we are very likely to notice that it wasn't a bad day either. For those days when the readings are negative, we would notice that our day did not go as bad as it was written on the paper; this is because our mind wasn't influenced by the negative information that we might have gotten if we had read it ourself in the morning.

- The horoscope is a very good analogy for compliments and criticisms, for just like positive and negative readings, they keep playing at the back of our minds. Immediately after we are complimented or criticized, especially by someone who is significant in our life (be it be our parents, siblings, best friend, or partner) we respond in a particular manner and the moment passes away. But very often those words actually continue to play in our subconscious and unconscious, and we are made to ponder, "Am I really like that?" Which more often than not, transforms into, "What if I really am like that?" And finally, it begins to make subtle reflections in our actions. In a similar fashion, the ball also rolls back to our court as well, for we too shall have opportunities to compliment or criticize others. So, when the time comes, make sure what you speak doesn't harm the other person; for like someone once said, words spoken once cannot be forgotten but only forgiven.

Voices in my Head (G)

Introduction

Self-talk is an integral element for our mental health, and whether the self-talk one has with themselves is positive or negative is a strong indicator of their mental state. A popular exercise used by therapists that uses this concept of self-talk is the Gestalt technique of "Empty Chair". This exercise draws many elements from the classical exercise, but unlike the Empty Chair technique, which is used in individual counselling settings, this activity is to be used in a group setting, and unlike the classical exercise, which focuses on both the interpersonal relationships and inner conflicts, this activity focuses solely on the internal dialogues. It is a powerful tool to generate insight into one's own inner world.

Most suitable context

Retreats or settings where it is essential/beneficial for the group members to know each other. Best suited for small groups.

Pre-requisite

- By the time the activity is done, the group members should be comfortable with each other and a sense of "safe space" should be established among them.

- The facilitator also needs to participate in this activity.

Preparation

Seat all the participants in a circular formation.

Instructions

1. I want all of you to think of something that you are planning to do; it can be anything from confessing to someone to an anger outburst to going on a trip to buying something to anything else. Think of a matter that you are comfortable sharing with the group.

2. Once you are done thinking of the matter that you shall share, one-by-one I want all of you to volunteer and come to the center of the circle.

3. Once at the center, imagine that you are planning in your mind but plan out loud.

4. For the rest, I want all of you to listen carefully to what the person at the center is speaking and strike a conversation with him/her as if you are part of the planning process, discuss all the details you want to.

5. As the larger group responds, the volunteer shall respond back and the conversation shall continue

       till either the group stops responding, or till I say so (ask them to stop after 10 minutes).

6. The same process shall continue till all of us have come to the center.

Note: If nobody volunteers, take the initiative to head to the center; this shall ease the tension among the participants.

Debrief

When we imagine a conversation in our mind, we tend to imagine possible outcomes or responses and compose multiple variants of the same conversation in our mind. It is also important to note here that when we engage in self-talk, we are highly influenced by the experiences and people we encounter; and hence if carefully observed upon, we realize that the voices in our self-talk are not only our own, but also of the people in our lives. What usually happens though is that we don't pay much attention to whose voice is being played in our mind, due to which it becomes difficult to recognize where a particular thought is arising from. What happened here was giving physical existence to the voices we are likely to hear when we are having a dialogue with ourselves; even though it may seem on the surface level that we are simply having a conversation with ourselves, but when observed on a deeper level, we realize that we are conversing with all those who have made an impact in our lives and in ways minor and major, shaped our thinking process.

Water Bag (G&O)

Introduction

Resilience is what helps us get up no matter how many times we fall; protects us from breaking. Often there are objects around us which we use for trivial purposes, but fail to realize the deep meanings it can teach us. In this activity, three simple objects are used to help the participant realize the importance of being resilient. This is an activity that can be done in both individuals as well as group settings.

Most suitable context

Workshops for building resilience and counselling sessions focusing on the need for self-improvement.

Prerequisite

A spot that can be safely made wet.

Materials

- Paper bag (1 per person)

- Balloon (1 per person)

- High quality plastic bag (1 per person)

- Water (2 liters per person)

Preparation

Hand the client/participants a paper bag, a balloon, and a plastic bag.

Instructions

1. First, start pouring water into the paper bag.

2. Continue pouring till it can take no more.

3. Now start pouring into the balloon.

4. Just like the paper bag, continue pouring till it gives in.

5. Now pour the rest of the water into the plastic bag.

Debrief

- What did you notice?

- As you can see, the paper bag gave in very shortly after being exposed to the water, and the balloon, even though it resisted by expanding and making space, but eventually it also gave in by exploding. However, the plastic bag, instead of making extra space, continued to expel the excess water from the top.

- These three are just like our levels of resilience; if we have poor levels of resilience, we will succumb to our adversities as easily as the paper bag. During the process of building resilience, we are like the balloon, where we fight and try to adjust to our adversities, however in this scenario even though we are much more resilient than the paper bag, but are still at risk of experiencing breakdowns. Finally, when we reach the level of plastic back, there is a sense of surrender that enables us to disconnect from anything that is toxic for our growth process and consciously expel the negativity from our lives.

- So, which level of resilience do you believe you are in currently?

Tower Defense (G)

Introduction

Trust is one of the most essential components of an effective team, however, our preconceived notions often act as a hindrance in the path of us trusting others. This is a competitive, but fun game to highlight the various dynamics of teams and how important it is to keep an open mind.

Most suitable context

Corporate or military-based workshops on teambuilding. Best suited for large groups.

Pre-requisite

Ample space for participants to freely move around.

Materials

A sheet of paper

Preparatory Instructions

1. The tallest members of the group please come forward and form a group of your own away from the larger group and me. You are group 1.

2. Members who are trouble makers, please come forward and form a group of your own away from the larger group, group 1, and me. You are group 2.

3. Members who are the most likely to be the first ones to help others, please come forward and form a group of your own away from the larger group, the other groups, and me. You are group 3.

4. The rest of you folks are group 4.

Procedural Instructions

1. Group 1, please come to me.

2. Take this sheet of paper. Your task is to create a tower and protect at all cost.

3. Group 2, please come to me.

4. Group 1 is creating a tower out of a sheet of paper, and your task is to ensure that they succeed in defending their tower from the others.

5. Group 3, please come to me.

6. Group 1 is going to defend a paper tower and your task is to take it down. You are allowed to resort to any means required for the task.

7. Group 4, please come to me.

8. Group 1 is going to defend a paper tower, while group 2 is going to help them, and group 3 is

going to attempt to destroy the tower. Your task is to distract the other groups from doing their tasks.

9. Group 1, once you all are ready, show a thumbs up and that would be the signal for the other groups to start with their tasks.

Debrief

- Group 3, how did it feel?

- Group 2, how did it feel?

- Group 1, how did it feel?

- Group 4, how did it feel?

- Often, we are pitted against opponents who have unfair advantages over us, the taller folks had over the attackers. But if we rely on teamwork, we can overcome it no matter what the adversity might be.

- How easy was it for group 1 to trust group 2 considering that they are known to be troublemakers?

- Often our judgment of others is colored by our preconceived notions, but if we are willing to look at them for who truly are and not what we know them to be like, it easier to place our trust in others.

- Group 4 was a representation of the various distractions that we experience on our journey.

Some distractions are attractive, while others are destructive, but both kinds are equally harmful, for they take us off track from our original goals. Individually it can at times be difficult to tackle these distractions, but with the help of friends and family, we can gain back our focus.

- Was it easier to cooperate within your group or to compete with the other groups?

- Please reflect on what made it easier to either cooperate or compete.

Break the Bottle (O&G)

Introduction

Breaking things on its own is cathartic, and when paired with visualization, it can prove to be quite a powerful experience. This exercise is primarily intended to facilitate a cathartic experience for people suffering from various forms of addiction since addiction involves intense amounts of pent-up thoughts and emotions. It is however to be kept in mind that caution needs to be practiced as this exercise involves the risk of injury from broken glass.

Most suitable context

This exercise is suitable for individual sessions for clients with addiction-related concerns, and for group work at deaddiction/rehabilitation centers.

Pre-requisite

If done in a group setting, it is advisable that the participants are seated in a circular formation on the ground.

Materials

Glass bottle (1 per person)

Instructions

1. Hold the bottle with both your hands and close your eyes.

2. Now try to remember when you (insert activity [e.g., drank]) for the first time.

3. Recollect all the emotions you felt back then.

4. Recollect all the thoughts that occurred to you back then.

5. Recollect all the feelings you usually feel whenever you (insert activity [e.g., drink]).

6. Now fill the bottle in your hands with all these thoughts and emotions.

7. It is ok if the bottle overflows.

8. Once you feel that there is nothing else to fill in the bottle, slowly open your eyes.

9. Now with all your might, smash the bottle on the floor in front of you (however be careful of the glass shards that will be released upon the breaking of the bottle).

Debrief

- How was the experience for you?

- Is there anything particular that you might want to share or express?

- If there is any discomfort that you might be experiencing, it would be a good idea to relax a little and take a few deep breaths.

Row, Row, Row Your Boat (G)

Introduction

Making paper boats is an activity that refreshes fond childhood memories for many of us; especially of sailing them on the puddles that formed on the roads after a heavy shower. This exercise adds a philosophical angle to the activity of making paper boats and reminds us about how it is not the resources one has that make the difference, but rather how one chooses to use them.

Most suitable context

Workshops on self-development and resource management

Materials

- A4 sheet of paper (one per person)

- A tub of water

Instructions

1. Tear your sheet of paper in half.

2. Make a paper boat out of one of the halves.

3. Put the unfolded paper on the tub of water.

4. Now put the paper boat on the tub of water.

Debrief

- What did you observe?

- Both the unfolded sheet of paper and the paper boat, were the same piece of paper to begin with and the paper boat did not receive any external additions apart from the folds.

- Usually, we find ourselves complaining that we don't have enough, but if we reflect, we realize that we do have similar resources as most around us.

- It is not what we have that makes the real difference, but rather what we do with all that we already have that actually makes the difference.

- We also need to bend and mold ourselves to achieve the optimum version of ourselves; a version that doesn't sink when released into the water.

- At the end of the day, we need to realize that what we are seeking outside, is usually within ourselves.

Boom! (G)

Introduction

Imagine a pressure cooker, now imagine what would happen if the whistle is prevented from blowing; it would explode, right? Our mind is just like that; it can contain thoughts and emotions up to a certain extent, beyond which it also can explode. This exercise draws an analogy from a popular activity; blowing balloons but with a twist.

Best suitable context

Workshops on communication and/or emotion management.

Materials

- Balloons (2 per person)

- Needle (1 per person)

Instructions

1. Blow one of the balloons and keep blowing till it bursts.

2. Use the needle to poke a couple of holes into the other balloon.

3. Now gently blow into the balloon.

4. Allow it to inflate but also allow time to deflate.

Debrief

- What difference did you observe between the two balloons? Apart from the obvious fact that the first one burst?

- The first balloon was pushed beyond the limits of its capacity.

- Whereas the second balloon had the luxury of release and wasn't rushed like the first one either.

- Often in our lives we keep bottling up thoughts and emotions, that burst out at the wrong time, and often in front of the wrong people.

- We also have tendency to often give in to the urge of getting things done as swiftly as possible; even though it is a reflection of efficient utilization of time, it can also lead to things being rushed.

- It is important to make conscious efforts not to let thoughts and emotions pile up within ourselves, but rather express and release whenever possible.

- At times social contexts force us to hold back, but during times like these we need to remind ourselves the risks we are putting ourselves in by bottling up our thoughts and emotions.

Blown Away (O&G)

Introduction

Communication is the key in any relationship, especially among people who stay together since they share their lives with each other. Through a little competitive game, this exercise stands as a metaphor for how important it is to not only communicate but also promote two-way communication in order for a relationship to sustain.

Most suitable context

Couple therapy for communication-related concerns or team-building workshops.

Preparation

Make the couple sit opposite to each other.

Materials

Paper ball (1 per couple)

Instructions

1. Place the paper ball right in the center in between the two of you.

2. Your objective is to blow over the ball onto the side of your partner.

3. Now on the count of three, both of you start blowing at the ball.

4. 1, 2, 3, blow!

Debrief

- What did you observe during the activity?

- In the beginning, the ball stayed at one place because both of you were blowing at the same time.

- Once the pace of your blowing changed, the ball started to move from one side to another.

- The paper ball represents the matter of discussion in any conversation.

- When we speak and express at the same time and with the same vigor, the conversation comes to a standstill as neither of us is able to understand the other in front of us.

- Whereas when we take turns to understand the other person, does the conversation move forward.

- However, when it comes to reaching to a conclusion, there is a need to come to an agreement; here since both of you were competitive, you were trying to get your point across, while trying to negate the other's point.

- When this happens, even if a conversation doesn't come to a standstill, it is fruitless as it is a mere consumption of time and energy for both.

- Every conversation doesn't necessarily need to come to a conclusion for some conversations are for the fun of it, but when an agreement is needed, it is necessary for one to be convinced of the other's point.

A Little Too Much (O&G)

Introduction

Soap is an essential commodity of any household or commercial place, but can a bar soap convey a message? This exercise is a metaphor for excess and how it is important to realize when we actually cross the line and enter the zone of "too much". A word of caution regarding this activity is that it should not lead to excessive wastage of water.

Most suitable context

Individual sessions on moving on and workshops on time management.

Materials

- A Bar of soap (1 per person)

- A washbasin or a bucket of water (1 per person)

Instructions

1. Take the bar of soap and start washing your hands.

2. Make sure you don't put the bar of soap down.

3. Continue washing your hands.

4. Drop the soap and wash your hands off the soap.

Debrief

- What are your observations and reflections from this activity?

- A bar of soap is an essential tool for washing our hands, but not putting the soap down prevented you from completing the process of washing your hands.

- **For moving on sessions:**Likewise, there are sweet memories, that provide us a feel-good experience. But if we hold on to them, we deprive ourselves of the chance of experiencing anything new, and, we can't complete the process of moving on. It is important to remember that those memories are like the bar of soap; important for us, but we can't continue to hold on to them if we want a fresh start. Yes, just like the bar of soap, we can revisit those memories for a healthy sense of nostalgia, but even if we do so, we ought to remind ourselves that we can't complete the process of washing our hands while holding the bar of soap.

- **For time management sessions:**Likewise, at times we find ourselves doing tasks that are important, but are not aligned to the primary task in hand. On the surface, it might not look like procrastination since we are not whiling away our time, but it is to be kept in mind that we are however deviating from the main task. This, if handled well, can prove to be multitasking, but multitasking is not always a good idea as there is a risk of compromise of quality and/or burnout. Holding on to the soap is also a metaphor for prolonging a task; we might not be deviating from our task, but we might be investing more time and energy than it demands. This might be due to a need for perfection, or a fear of failure, or any other reason, but regardless of the reason behind the act, it is important to be conscious about our actions and intentions.

Multi-Colored (O&G)

Introduction

The Gestalt and Psychoanalytic schools may be seen as distinct and unrelated approaches, since one focuses on the present moment, while the other emphasizes the past experiences. But this exercise, through the use of everyday items like handkerchiefs, watercolors, and water, blends the two and highlights an eclectic approach to these two contrasting schools of thought.

Most suitable context

Individual counselling sessions or workshops on self-esteem, and moving on.

Materials

- Handkerchief (4 per person)

- Tubes of watercolors (4 shades per person)

- A glass of water (1 per person)

- Empty glass (1 per person)

Instructions

1. Apply some color on one of the handkerchiefs.

2. Keeping the colored side facing the inside the glass, place the handkerchief on the mouth of the empty glass.

3. Slowly pour 1/4th of the water over it.

4. Repeat this procedure for the remaining handkerchiefs and remaining colors; pouring 1/4th of the water each time.

Debrief

- What did you notice?

- Did all the water get transferred from the first glass to the other?

- What happened to the color of the water?

- Can the water be brought back to its original state of colorlessness? Or separate one color from the other?

- We start as the colorless water, but our experiences color us, and with every experience, different shades continue to get added.

- It is important to remember that who we are at this moment is because of all of our experiences (big or small) in the past.

- Even if we try, we can't separate the past experiences from our present being, just as we can't transform the water back to its original form of colorlessness.

- Not only has all the experiences blended with each other as the colors did, but what we remember of them is also the information that has passed on from the memories of our unconscious mind (represented by the handkerchiefs that retained a certain amount of water from the first glass).

- What we can do, is accept the totality of our being, with all of our past experiences and future possibilities.

- Scientifically, we can transform the water back to its colorless form through evaporation and condensation, but the water wouldn't have the nuances of any of the combinations and permutations of the colors that were part of it formerly.

- Likewise, even if we manage to revert back to our past selves, we would miss out on all of our experiences (including the positive ones) and learnings.

- We are multi-layered and multi-colored, but that is what makes us, us.

Connect With Us

Thank you for becoming a part of our dream! If you share this dream of ours, and/or want to connect with us for one-on-one sessions or workshops, you can reach out to us through the following means of communication:

Website: www.whaterr.com
Mail: support@whaterr.com
Instagram: @whaterrsolutions
Facebook: @ whaterrdotcom
Pinterest: @whaterr_cares
Phone/WhatsApp: +91 95387 55515

Or if you happen to be in Bangalore, drop by at:
No 47, Royal Meridian Layout, 4th Cross Road, Behind St.Francis School, Bangalore, Karnataka, India, 560068

Glossary

- **Addiction (42):**Any form of behavior that becomes a pattern or a loop that causes a sense of discomfort (physical, emotional, and psychological) when one tries to exit from it. Addictive behavior is not limited to any substance but can also extend to people, places, objects, emotions, or experiences.

- **Anger (1):**Anger is a natural response to any form of discomfort, however, if not regulated, it can escalate into outbursts that can cause physical and/or emotional harm to self or people and objects around oneself.

- **Anger Management (1):**The skills and techniques used to regulate and channelize one's anger in the right direction.

- **Communication (1, 21, 28, 46, 48):**The process whereby one uses certain verbal or non-verbal symbols to express their thoughts and feelings, and in turn these symbols are received, processed, and responded to by the other.

- **Empathy (21):**The ability to objectively understand what the other person is going through (without getting entangled in the web of emotions), and provide the necessary support (if needed).

- **Emotion Management (5, 46):**The ability to appropriately use the right emotions according to the demands of the circumstances.

- **Goal Setting (11):**The process of planning and setting up goals that one wishes to achieve over a period of time.

- **Interpersonal Issues (25):**Concerns and grievances an individual might have with another individual or group of individuals on various fronts ranging from disagreements, to miscommunication, to violation of boundaries, to multiple other concerns.

- **Moving On (50, 53):**The process of coming to terms with the incidences in one's life and engaging in a healthy lifestyle that is not negatively impacted by the concerned incident(s) (usually by undergoing the five stages of loss proposed by Elisabeth Kubler-Ross [1969], i.e., denial, anger, bargaining, depressions, and acceptance).

- **Planning (11):**The process of understanding the goals one has in hand and evaluate whether they are SMART (Specific, Measurable, Achievable,

Realistic, and Time-bound) goals, before putting them down on a schedule.

- **Problem Solving (1, 15, 17, 19):** The ability to navigate through difficult situations by either directly addressing the problem at hand, and/or seeking the assistance of others.

- **Relationship Management (1):** The ability to navigate through interpersonal issues, and work towards building/maintaining a long-lasting and fulfilling relationship.

- **Resilience (36):** The ability to bounce back after a setback (major or minor) one experiences and continue striving to reach their goals.

- **Resistance (21):** The unwillingness of an individual to move forward on the path of healing and self-development.

- **Resource Management (44):** The ability to optimally utilize available resources to ensure maximum, productive output.

- **Self-Control (15):** The ability to regulate our thoughts and emotions, to achieve situation-appropriate behavior.

- **Self-Development (36, 44):** The process of working towards becoming one's best possible version of themselves.

- **Self-Esteem (5, 53):**An individual's personal evaluation of themselves, and what they believe they deserve.

- **Subliminal Perception (31):**The process whereby the stimuli one is exposed to influences their thought patterns without their conscious realization.

- **Team Building (13, 15, 17, 21, 28, 33, 39, 48):**The process of bringing together a group of people for achieving a common goal, ensuring a strong bonding process among the members, and working towards setting a common goal.

- **Time Management (50):**The process of ensuring optimum utilization of time while taking into consideration the tasks one has in hand.